Hexagons

Teddy Borth

Abdo
SHAPES ARE FUN!
Kids

abdopublishing.com

Published by Abdo Kids, a division of ABDO, PO Box 398166, Minneapolis, Minnesota 55439.
Copyright © 2016 by Abdo Consulting Group, Inc. International copyrights reserved in all countries.
No part of this book may be reproduced in any form without written permission from the publisher.

Printed in the United States of America, North Mankato, Minnesota.

102015
012016

Photo Credits: Getty Images, iStock, Shutterstock

Production Contributors: Teddy Borth, Jennie Forsberg, Grace Hansen

Design Contributors: Candice Keimig, Dorothy Toth

Library of Congress Control Number: 2015941976

Cataloging-in-Publication Data

Borth, Teddy.
 Hexagons / Teddy Borth.
   p. cm. -- (Shapes are fun!)
ISBN 978-1-68080-143-9 (lib. bdg.)
Includes index.
1. Hexagons--Juvenile literature. 2. Geometry--Juvenile literature. 3. Shapes--Juvenile literature.   I. Title.
516--dc23
                    2015941976

Table of Contents

Hexagons

A hexagon has 6 sides.

It has 6 angles.

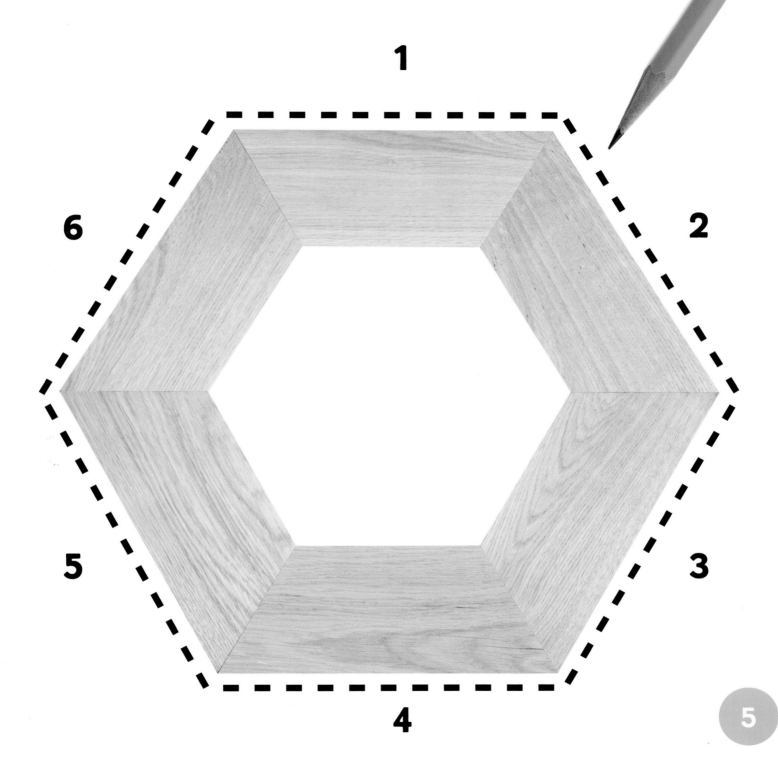

This shape is found all over!

Bees use them.

Bees keep honey in them.

They are on a soccer ball.

Todd counts all the white ones.

They are on the floor.

They can be colorful.

They are on turtles.

They help make the shell strong.

They are the shape of pencils.

They will not roll away!

16

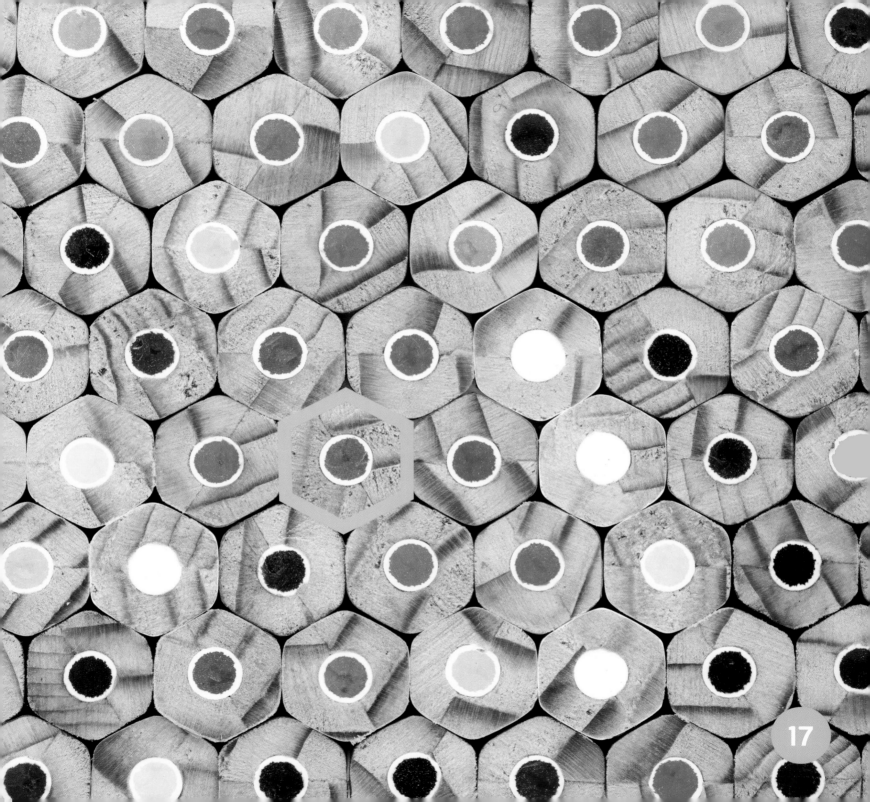

Hex nuts can be really big! You turn them with the right tool.

Look around you!

You will find a hexagon.

Count the Hexagons!

Glossary

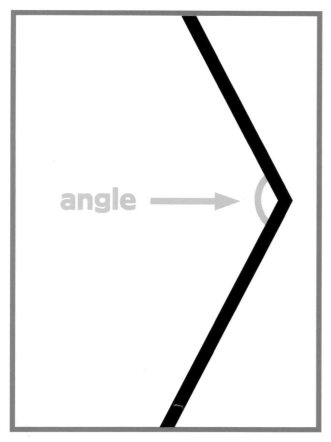

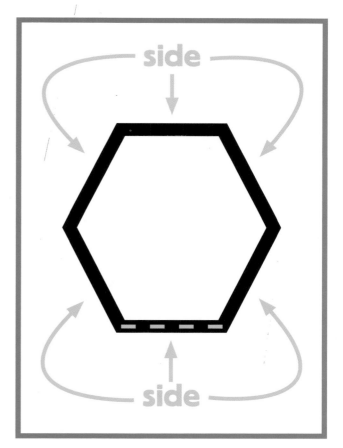

angle
a figure formed by two lines
extending from the same point.

side
a line forming a border of
an object.

Index

abdokids.com

Use this code to log on to abdokids.com and access crafts, games, videos, and more!

Abdo Kids Code:
SHK1439